All in the Family

by Tara McCarthy

Orlando Boston Dallas Chicago San Diego

Visit *The Learning Site!*
www.harcourtschool.com

What kinds of things can family members do together? Family members can play sports together. Venus and Serena Williams are sisters who play tennis together as a team. Their hard work has won them many medals and trophies.

Family members can have adventures together. Laura Ingalls Wilder wrote wonderful books about her adventures with her family. Her daughter helped her write the books.

Family members can learn from each other. Martin Luther King Jr. learned from his father, Martin Luther King Sr., that words are important. Both men used words to make big changes.

Family members can work and have fun together. That is what the Marx brothers did. They made movies and made many people laugh.

Family members can invent things together. The Wright brothers worked hard to make their dream of flying a reality.

Read on to find out more about these family members.

Two Special Sisters

Serena and Venus Williams are sisters. They are also good friends. Venus is almost two years older than her sister Serena. The sisters are very close to each other. They're not just close because they are sisters. They are close because they both play tennis.

The Williams sisters both went to the 2000 Olympics in Sydney, Australia. They both won gold medals in women's tennis.

Venus won a women's singles title. That means she played tennis against another player. Venus and Serena won the women's doubles title together. That means they played as a team against two players on another team. Venus became the second woman ever to win both a singles and a doubles title in the Olympics.

The Williams sisters made history earlier that year. They were the first sisters to win a doubles title. They would go on to win two more! In 1998 Serena Williams won her first Grand Slam title at the U.S. Open. Venus won her first Grand Slam title the next year.

Everyone wondered what would happen if the sisters had to play each other. Venus and Serena didn't want to play each other in a tournament. They took turns playing, so they wouldn't have to play against each other. Finally, in 2000, the sisters had to play against each other. Venus won.

Venus was named Sportswoman of the Year by *Sports Illustrated* magazine.

Serena is the second African American woman ever to win the U.S. Open. Venus is the second African American woman to win Wimbledon. Althea Gibson was the first. Althea Gibson won her Grand Slam titles in 1958.

How the sisters look also has made them popular. They are both very tall, and they wear bright clothing. Sometimes the two sisters braid beads into their hair.

The two sisters also do advertisements for makeup and television commercials for sports clothing. Both sisters want to be role models for young girls.

Family Adventures

Many years ago, Charles and Caroline Ingalls moved to Wisconsin and started a farm. They built a house. There were very few cities and towns in this part of the country. There were very few people, houses, and roads.

The Ingalls soon had two daughters. Their names were Mary and Laura. As children, Mary and Laura learned how to work on their farm. They helped in the fields, and they did chores.

Later the family moved. This time they went to Kansas. Kansas was mostly a prairie. This new place was very different from Wisconsin. Then the family

moved again, first to Minnesota, then to the Dakota Territory. Every place they went, the family had to build a new house and start a new farm. Life was hard, but the family worked together. Each move was a new adventure.

Laura Ingalls wrote about her family and her adventures. She wanted to turn her notes into a good book someday.

Years later when Laura was about sixty years old, she asked her daughter Rose to help her. Laura's daughter Rose was a very good writer and liked helping her mother. Rose learned so much from reading her mother's notes and from talking to her.

Laura and Rose worked together. Slowly they rewrote Laura's notes to make stories. They finished their first book, and many people enjoyed reading it. Together Laura and Rose wrote more books. Laura's stories became very popular.

Father and Son Preachers

Martin Luther King Jr. learned many things from his parents. His mother was a schoolteacher. His father was a preacher at a local church.

Martin Luther King Sr. helped people in the community. Young Martin watched his father defend the rights of others. He wanted to help people just like his father did.

Martin Luther King Jr. also learned from the way his father spoke. His father was a Baptist preacher and a great speaker. His father talked about freedom for all Americans and how to respect others. He admired his father and hoped to be like him one day.

Martin Luther King Jr. went to school to be a preacher just like his father. When he was eighteen years old, he became a minister at his father's church.

Martin Luther King Jr. used words to help African Americans fight for their rights. He used words to get other people to help. Martin Luther King Jr. tried to teach what he had learned from his father to other people.

Martin Luther King Jr. told people to be kind to each other. He wanted all people to be treated equally. He wanted all Americans to have the same rights.

Martin Luther King Jr. and his father.

Martin Luther King Jr. went on marches and gave famous speeches. In 1963 Martin Luther King, Jr. led 200,000 people in Washington, D.C., on a march for equal rights.

Martin Luther King Jr. followed his father in many ways. He learned how to be a good speaker, and he helped change the world with his words.

Five Funny Brothers

Sometimes families have fun together. The five Marx brothers had fun together. They wanted to be like their mother, Minnie Marx. Minnie acted on a stage. When they were young, the Marx brothers put on plays together. When they grew up, they made movies together.

Just for fun, the Marx brothers changed their names. Arthur changed his name to Harpo. Julius changed his name to Groucho. Leonard changed his name to Chico. Milton changed his name to Gummo. Herbert changed his name to Zeppo.

At first the five brothers performed together. Gummo had other interests, though, and he found another job.

Harpo wore an old hat and a long coat. His hair was blond and curly. His shoes were big, like a clown's shoes. Harpo made people think that he couldn't talk. Sometimes Harpo would sneak up on people and beep a horn that he hid in his coat. Sometimes Harpo would play the harp.

Chico mixed up his words. He might say a "fig ban" instead of a "big fan." He might say "gets low" instead of "let's go." Sometimes people didn't know what Chico was saying, but they thought that he was very funny.

Groucho acted like the only smart brother. He got the other brothers into trouble. Then he would get them out of trouble. He would tell his brothers what to do. He wore a big mustache and made lots of jokes.

At first, the Marx brothers acted on a stage. After some success, the Marx brothers were starring in movies. Zeppo was in five of the movies. Then he found another job, too.

Then there were just three Marx brothers in the movies—Groucho, Harpo, and Chico. They made many more funny movies together. *The Cocoanuts, Animal Crackers, Monkey Business, Duck Soup,* and *Horse Feathers* are just some of the movies they made.

Finally, Groucho Marx was the only star left. He had a TV quiz show called *You Bet Your Life.* Groucho asked contestants questions, and if they got the answer right, a chicken came down over their heads!

Two Determined Brothers

Sometimes brothers work together to invent things. A hundred years ago, flying in a plane was just a dream. Two brothers decided to make the dream a reality. The brothers were Wilbur and Orville Wright.

When they were little boys, the Wright brothers always did everything together. They liked to take things apart and put things back together again. They liked to see how things worked.

In 1896 the Wright brothers heard about a man named Otto Lilienthal. Lilienthal made and flew hang gliders. The Wright brothers were interested in Lilienthal's work. They read about flying. They decided to build a glider, too.

In 1900 Orville and Wilbur took their glider to Kill Devil Hill in Kitty Hawk, North Carolina. There they tried out the glider. It didn't work well. Neither did the one they built in 1901.

The Wright brothers learned more about how to build wings. They learned more about wind, and they built new gliders.

In 1902 they took the new glider to the hill in North Carolina. This was their third try. This third glider worked best of all. The brothers made more than 1,000 glides in it. Some of the glides went more than 600 feet. That might not seem very far today. But more than a hundred years ago, it was really amazing!

Of course the Wright Brothers wanted to fly more than 600 feet. To do that, they needed a plane that had power. The plane needed an engine, or something to make it go forward. It also needed something to make it go up in the air.

In December 1903 Orville and Wilbur built their first real airplane. They named it the *Flyer I*. It had a gasoline engine. It weighed 605 pounds and was 21 feet long.

Flyer I's first flight did not go well. But after a few more tries, it did fine. The longest flight lasted 59 seconds. The plane traveled 852 feet. Only five other people were there to see the flight. Most people didn't believe the Wright brothers had made a plane that could fly. There were no reports about the flight until March 1904.

Orville and Wilbur made more planes. *Flyer III* could turn, circle, and even do figure eights. The plane could stay up as long as the gas lasted. On October 5, 1905, Wilbur flew *Flyer III* for 39 minutes. He traveled about 24 miles.

The news about *Flyer III* traveled all over the world. Soon the whole world wanted to see what the Wright brothers would do next.